SOON TO BE MRS

A GUIDE ON PREPARING YOURSELF TO BE A WIFE

MELANIE K FERNANDEZ

SOON TO BE MRS

Copyright © 2018 by Melanie K Fernandez

All right reserved. In accordance with the U.S. Copyright Acts of 1976, No part of this publication may be reproduced, distributed or transmitted in any form or by other electronic or mechanical method without prior expressed permission of the author, except in the case of brief quotations embodied in critical reviews and other commercial uses permitted by copyright laws.

Thank you for your support of the author's rights.

Author by Melanie K Fernandez

CONTENTS

PREPARATION-1 1

PREPARATION-2 4

GUIDANCE 6

PURPOSE/CALLING 8

SINGLE MOTHERS 11

FAITH & THE SPIRIT OF EXPECTATION 16

HOW TO AVOID HEARTACHE 18

SOUL TIES 21

CELIBACY 24

COMMIT TO THE PROCESS 27

SUBMISSION 30

DID GOD SAY HE'S YOUR HUSBAND 33

PREPARATION-1

It sounds easier said than done right? *"Prepare yourself to be a wife," or anything you pray for, you must prepare for,"* (spoken by the very talented and anointed brother in Christ, Mr. Devon Franklin). Although very true, it can be confusing to anyone who hasn't heard this spoken before. So, what does that mean exactly? To prepare one's self to be a wife, it means to take the time to allow God to educate you on who you are, as a wife. God will also use different means and many ways to inform you of what He wants you to know. Whether that is through reading books or watching YouTube videos on preparing to be a wife; God will always guide you.

Therefore, it is so important to have a relationship with God first. Only He can direct your paths. God wants you to let Him lead you and be your life; not just be a part of it. In doing so, He can show you anything, especially if the man that you're currently with, is your husband or not; because the man that God has ordained for you to be with, was made just for you since the beginning of time. Unfortunately, this is still difficult for some men and women to grasp.

It is hard for some to consider that God our creator, who made the heavens and earth, the moon and the stars, and of course, all mankind; to believe that He would have anything to do with choosing our forever mates. Yes, that God! Our Father who should not be put into some box; confining or restricting what He is able to do. This false idea, created by Christians, that God is unable or simply doesn't care enough to reveal to us, who our spouses are even bring them, when the time is right. Let's get rid of this misconception of God and trust and know that *"now to him who is able to do exceedingly and abundantly above all that we ask or think, according to the power that works in us." (ESV) (Ephesians 3:20-21).*

Preparing yourself to be a wife is something that is necessary for anyone looking forward to marriage. Cultivating a strong relationship with God should be first on the list; it is through Him that you will even be with the right person. Preparation is key.

Here are 3(three) tips that you need to establish before asking God to bring to you your husband.

- ❖ *Who am I? :* You should know who you are before considering marriage. Asking God is the only way to know. By spending time with Him, He will reveal to you who you are in Christ. *"Keep on asking, and you will receive what you ask for. Keep on seeking, and you will find. Keep on knocking, and the door will be opened to you"* (NLT) (Mathew 7:7).

- ❖ *Know your purpose*: It is important to know what you are put on this earth to do. What is your mission? If you do not know what your mission is, then how are you going to help your husband with his? (I talk more about this in chapter 3)

- ❖ *Prayer Life*: I can't stress enough that you have to pray, pray, and pray. What is your prayer life like? Before God brings your soul mate into your life, you should be praying and covering your husband.

PREPARATION-2

In preparing to be a wife, it is important to know our role as single women of God and what that really means. We do not become wives after we say, "I do." No, that is a misconception that some women still have. Being keepers of the home, it is important to know and to do the things that a wife does before we get married. Cooking and cleaning are things that as a woman, you should be preparing to do, before God brings you your husband.

If you do not know how to cook, then you are not ready to be a wife. Now, being able to cook a five-course meal is not what I mean; however, in this day and time, there is really no excuse for both men and women, to not know how to cook; if you have the means to do it. I believe that a man should also learn to cook before he considers marriage, but I won't get into that.

When I first started out, I only knew the basics; cooking eggs, rice, or frying meat; but then I started watching cooking shows non-stop and reading cook books. By then, I already had my first child, so that helped and motivated me in the right direction to wanting to learn more about cooking. Living in a clean home is not only necessary, but when your home is clean, studies have shown that people are much happier coming home to a clean one. If we as women of God are asking Him for a husband, then we undoubtedly need to make sure we know how to keep our homes not only clean, but as a place of peace for our family. Doing this and continually doing these things, is preparation for what we are praying for.

From what God has shown me and from my own experience, no man wants to come home to a dirty house. Now, with all this being said, I believe that a man should know how to clean also; but much of the time, as women, it is our responsibility to be keepers of our home, and to make sure it is a place of peace.

GUIDANCE

Guidance from God, is like a dance. He wants to lead and order every step that you take. We live in a world today where we don't take the time to hear from Him. Some of us don't even sit before God and ask Him for instruction, nor do we wait to hear what He has to say. It is not enough to pray for guidance; but we should also pray and then wait on the Lord to speak to us. *"Call to me and I will answer you, and will tell you great and hidden things that you have not known."* (ESV) (Jeremiah 33:3).

God is waiting to reveal things we need to know and more; especially the man of God, that He created just for us. Being led by God's Holy Spirit is so important. By asking the Lord for wisdom or to lead you, and to help you through life; God uses His Holy Spirit to do this. It is our guide; our Helper. Jesus says in *John 14:16-17*, *"And I will ask the Father, and he will give you another Helper, to be with you forever, even the Spirit of truth, whom the world can not receive, because it neither sees him nor knows him. You know him, for he dwells with you and will be in you."* For those of you that do not have the Holy Spirit, it is vital that you press into God, and ask Him to receive his Holy Spirit, which is a gift. *"If you ask me anything in my name, I will do it." (ESV) (John 14:4).* Having God in our lives and constantly asking and allowing Him to show us what to do, for every and anything, is key.

PURPOSE/CALLING

What has God called you to do? What this means is simply this; what is your mission that God intends for you to fulfill before Christ returns? To be clear, we all have purposes, gifts and talents; our job as Christians, is to spread the gospel and bring people into the knowledge of Christ. Now, the difference in purpose between us as Christians, is how God wants each one of us to use our gifts. God specifically made us all unique and He intended for us to use our gifts and talents in the way that He called us to do it.

We are all uniquely formed in Christ's image and different from everyone else, but our mission will always be the same. God made us to fill a very special need in this world and no one else can do it in the way that each one of us was created to do it. It is your destiny, your gift, your inheritance, to make effective use of it, to spread the gospel to God's people. For me, God has called me to create; in doing so, He told me to write books and movies, and to start my own businesses. Now, after I took that first step in writing my first book (journal), titled, "Longing for Him," that is when God revealed to me that He wanted more from me. He told that He wanted me to write books. See, because I was obedient to what God told me to do; overtime He showed me more and gave me more opportunities to receive more from Him and create more for Him. *"Everyone to whom much was much given, of him much will be required, and from him to whom they entrusted much, they will demand the more."* (ESV) (Luke 12:48)

Ladies, when you are in your purpose, doing what God has told you to do, you will be whole and filled with so much joy because you are doing the will of our Father and being in His will, is the best place to be. See, God is a God of sequence; He wants you to take that first step into what He has called you to do; that first step into your destiny. Only after being obedient and taking that initial step, will God give you the next step of your journey. God loves every one of us and He only wants what's best for us; that's why it is so important for us to listen to what He is telling us to do and He will lead us on the right path.

SINGLE MOTHERS

To all my sisters in Christ, I want to congratulate you on being a mom because it is in my own opinion, the hardest job in all the earth, period. So, thank you!

Now, being a single parent is very hard, and there is nothing like being a mother. From my own experience, it is very exhausting in every way. Even while being a stay-at-home mom, it is very tiring, mentally, physically, and emotionally. As mothers, we are our children's nurse, psychiatrist, mediator, teacher, maid, cook etc. Without the Holy Spirit's help, I couldn't be any of those things. With faith through Jesus, I can be the best mom that I can be, and that is all we can do. There is no such thing as being a perfect mom; there is such thing as being the best version of ourselves, and God knows that everyday isn't going to be about rainbows and butterflies; but that instead of letting the everyday stress get to us, we are praying and asking God to help us.

It's a simple and easy thing to say to God, to please help me right now. It takes two seconds to open our mouths and just speak to the Lord. I believe that sometimes we tend to overthink just talking to God. For instance, when I am stressed from dealing with my kids and I am upset that I have had to tell them to do something more than three times, I have learned to stop what I was doing, and just give it to God; I would say please Lord give me patience with these kids because I need you right now; and God will do what you ask if you believe it. *"Ask and you shall receive"* (Mathew 7:7).

Instead of yelling , screaming or spanking our kids most of the time, we should take a few seconds and ask for help, and the Lord will. Now, I do believe in spanking my kids, when it is necessary and not for any little thing. Take more time and just ask the Lord for guidance and how to be a better mom and the best mom that we can be for our children. As parents, we should never assume that "we got this," or because this is how I was raised, this is how I am going to raise my children; no, let God show you how He wants you to raise your kids, because God in His infinite wisdom, knows what's best for us all.

Time and time again, God had proven Himself to me, through the little things, so that I can trust Him with the bigger things. He is truly amazing in everything that He does.

Now, being a single mom while preparing to be a wife, is part of the journey. Like I've said before, there is no such thing as being the perfect mom; she doesn't exist; so, with that being said, do not think that you must be perfect, or have all your stuff together before God presents you to your husband. Listen, you will be as prepared as much as God wants you to be.

Every woman of God is different; therefore, God deals with each one of us accordingly. Don't assume that because another sister in Christ only had to do one to three things to prepare herself to be a wife, and you had to do twelve different processes before becoming a wife, that you think the one with less to do, isn't really prepared. Since we are all in various stages in life and in our walk with Christ, it is up to the Father to determine what we need in order to do anything. God loves us all the same; so, let us focus on that and pray for each other that God will send us our future husbands, when God says we are ready.

For me, as a single mom, when I am praying to God, I am always praying that my future husband will love my children as his own; but also, that he will see them as God sees them, and he will love them as God loves them. This is also what I pray for over me; that my future husband will love me as Christ loves the church and that he will see me as God does, and vice versa. I also pray that he will be kind, compassionate, passionate, loyal, loving, affectionate, romantic, etc. With all that being said, it is also important to ask God to reveal your future husband's heart to you.

Now, how he will look is not that important, granted, God will not bring us someone that we wouldn't find attractive; however, God will always use the Spirit of that person to attract you; not his looks. Making all your requests known to God is important, but also what you would want in your future husband. Now ladies, when you are making a list or if you have already made one, it is important to focus on the man's character; his insides, his heart. God of course already knows what kind of man we need; as such, he has already been picked out for us since creation was formed. However, prayer changes everything and praying for your future husband now, will make a difference in the future.

FAITH & THE SPIRIT OF EXPECTATION

"Now faith is the assurance of things hoped for, the conviction of things not seen." (Hebrews 11:1) What are you believing God for? Do you believe that God is going to bring you and your future husband together, or are you doubting and complaining to God about when is it going to happen for me? See, God wants us to know and not doubt that He will give us the desires of our hearts no matter what; and He wants to do this; (why you might ask), because God is the One who put those desires in our hearts to begin with. Sometimes, what God wants for us, is those desires in our hearts. If you strongly desire to be married, then continue to pray to God for guidance and Him to prepare your heart for your ordained husband; and when you pray, know that it is going to happen.

Expecting something to happen that God has already told you will happen, or something that He has purposely placed in your heart, is necessary. Having the Spirit of expectancy, is simply having a knowing in your spirit that God can and will do the miraculous in your life, and the impossible. God will do anything you ask Him to do, if you have the faith and it is in alignment with what He wants for your life.

HOW TO AVOID HEARTACHE

Waiting for the right one that God has for you, is key. Do not date. Why? Because dating is worldly; and when you seek God concerning this, it will be clearer to you why. In today's world, some of us know that dating is spending a little or a lot of time with someone, in order to find out if he/she is the "one" or not. In other cases, dating is just another form of having fun (having sex), because he/she knows that they are not ready for a monogamous relationship and dating for them is really a void they're filling. Whichever the reason, dating was not created for us as Christ followers. It is so important to really seek and ask God any and everything for wisdom and discernment.

Think about it; when we ask God who our husbands are, and when He reveals this to us, it cuts out all that dating stuff away because there's no need for it. It is that simple. Having a relationship with God is not complicated by any means. Just ask the Lord, and He will tell you; He wants to tell you these things. Ladies, you do not have to wait for a man to say, *"Well, let me see if she is the one,"* or vice versa. Dating is all about *"well, let me see if he/she is the one."* See, by asking God and seeking Him, He will reveal who He has for you; and you can avoid dead-end relationships, and therefore heartache. When you start a relationship with a man, without consulting God first, then you are just setting yourself up for future failure. Not only that but you are wasting God's time and yours.

God wants to bring you the man that He made just for you; before He even formed you; however, He can't do that if there is already a man in his place. If there is a man that you are seeing at any stage and God did not tell you or show you that this is your husband, then that man that you are keeping around you, is just taking up the space that your future husband should be in. Then, when you finally decide to end the relationship, now God has to take more time healing you and delivering you from all the hurt and pain that most women end up having from a break-up.

We as women need to focus on God and what He wants us to do in every area in our lives. I promise you, this will save you extra heartache and wasted time that could have been spent on preparing and positioning yourself to be a wife. Now, I am not saying that we will not go through some things and through tests and trials, but praying and asking God first, will prevent a lot of the unnecessary pain we put ourselves through by doing what we want to do instead of what God wants us to do.

SOUL TIES

What is a soul tie? A soul tie is a spiritual bond between people; and that soul tie or soul ties, can either be a good thing or terrible thing. If you are spiritually tied to the wrong person(s), then it is imperative that you seek and ask God to break it! How do you know if you are spiritually tied to the right person?

Its quiet easy, If you are married to one that God has ordained for you, then that is the only soul tie that should remain. Since a soul tie, ties two souls together, (or more) in the spiritual realm, it is important to know what can happen after giving your body to someone who is not your ordained mate. When you have sex with someone other than your ordained spouse, then you are opening yourself up to demonic spirits that are attached to that person. These are called unholy soul ties that serve as bridges between people who are sharing back and forth their demonic garbage. For example, when a woman gets involved with a man, and they end up having sex, then the two of you have just created a soul tie; furthermore, if this man is abusive to you in any way, then you will find yourself going back to him; why? Because now you've created a soul tie with this man and you're constantly trying to figure out why do you feel so connected to him, or why do you keep going back to him when he is treating you like dirt.

My sisters and brothers in Christ, it is these soul ties that have a spiritual hold on you, but you must break free by asking God. He wants to break the chains of a soul tie(s), but you need to ask for forgiveness and ask to break these soul ties that you yourself have created. *1Corinthians 6:16 says, "Or do you not know that he who is joined to a prostitute becomes one body with her? For, as it is written, the two shall become one flesh."* This is a prime example of what happens after sexual intercourse with someone; both souls intertwine and become one, along with all the spiritual baggage attached to that one person or persons. Asking and allowing God to break those soul ties, is something that we all need healing from, and only then can we be free from this form of sexual bondage; through Jesus Christ.

CELIBACY

Is God telling you to be celibate? You should know that if God is calling you to be celibate, it is for your own good. God will not bring you your spouse if you are having sex with someone. Let's be honest, how can God bless you with the man, if you are allowing the wrong man, to take his place? It's not going to happen. If you are in this situation, then please ask God to give you the strength and the courage to let that man go. Ladies, it is time to let him go and never look back. I hear the Lord saying, "It is time. It is your time; it is your season for a new thing." Yes Lord, hallelujah praise God Almighty!

Being celibate is not the same as abstinence. When someone decides to remain abstinence from having sex, it is usually to take a break from it; with no real goal at the end of it. Abstinence is something that one has decided to abstain from, for their own personal gain. When someone makes the decision to become celibate, it is for spiritual reasons; it is to accomplish a goal, and to go deeper into your relationship with Christ. Celibacy is intentional, and it is also a commitment; not only to God, but to purity itself. You are purifying yourself when you are not having sex outside of marriage.

This what God has always intended for His people since the beginning; choosing to be celibate and remain celibate until God brings to you your purpose mate. This is honoring God and living in the life that He intended for you; but being celibate also honors your own body, because your body is God's temple. See, celibacy is so much more than making a commitment to wait until marriage before having sex; it brings you closer to God because you have more clarity now, then you ever had before. We as women, by nature, are emotional; and if we are not careful, we will make decisions based off our emotions and how we feel, and emotional decisions are always dangerous. So, keep in mind that celibacy is by no means easy; the struggle is real, but by continuously asking and seeking God to help you not to stumble, and setting your mind on what God has purposed for you to do, will keep you on the right path.

Remember, the Lord will never steer you down the wrong path, and His plans are always for your own good. Make the decision to become celibate, whether you are a virgin or not, make this a commitment to God and yourself; and I promise you, it will change your life forever.

COMMIT TO THE PROCESS

The process, is a series of events that must take place before the promise Understanding this will really help to know why we're going through what we're going through. Staying committed to the process without unwavering faith, is necessary. Remember, it's a process. When we're in a storm, and it feels like death, or when we can't see a way out; that is when our faith is being tested, but we must trust in the One who sees us there. When we are praying and crying out to God and it feels like He is not there or it feels like He has turned His back on us; sisters, know and believe in your heart that He is right there, because He is.

I am only speaking from experience, so I know exactly how these feels. I have said many times, *"God, where are you?"* It felt like God had abandoned me; and left me to figure things out for myself; and in those times, I would go to my bible and read His word and be reminded of what God says to us in times of trouble. *"The LORD himself goes before you and will be with you; he will never leave you nor forsake you. Do not be afraid; do not be discouraged."* After reading His word repeatedly and meditating on it day and night, that is what kept me from falling into despair; that is what kept me from giving up on God.

Despite my pain going through the unknown, lost and confused, I pushed through. I eventually started to tell myself daily that whatever God has for me on the other side of this, must be huge because of the hell that I am going through right now. When God tests us, it is not because He is angry with us or He likes to see us in pain; no, it is never that! It is because He has already seen our triumph over the enemy; over the storm. He has seen our victory in overcoming these tests and trials and knows that if we are putting our faith and trust in Him, then there is nothing that we can't overcome. See, we have to go through the process, or we can never reach the promise and what God has for us; whether that is your husband, owning your own business (es), or becoming an author, it's a process.

Everything that God has purposed for your life, it is a process.

SUBMISSION

Submission: Submitting and getting under the mission that God has appointed to your husband, for your ministry together. This is one of the meanings of being submissive to your husband. Now, for us as single women, who are preparing to be a wife, learning and accepting to be submissive to others, before you get married; this will allow you to transition easier into your role as a wife. Being submissive is another big part of becoming a wife. Remember, we do not become wives after we say, *"I do,"* no, we are to seek God and He will make us wives through our character, before we walk down the aisle. When you are submissive to God and talking to God and asking Him questions; just spending that necessary time with Him is essential; then God can use you.

See, it is all about having a relationship with God; not religion, a relationship. Only then can you even begin finding out who you are really are in

Christ and from there, you can walk into who and what God has called you to do.

In order to teach those who need to learn how to submit, God will always put people in your path to show and teach you what you need to learn. For example, if God has told you that He wants you to work somewhere and after working there for sometime, you might start to feel unappreciated or misunderstood by your co-workers, or even your boss, that you forget why God placed you there in the first place. If the Lord has placed you there, it is always for a reason. He is trying to teach you something.

From my own experience, it was usually submission and trust issues that God has been working on me, to free me from. While working at various jobs, for me, I had issues with submitting to women who were my bosses because I didn't trust women due to past hurt and pain. For every person, it will always be different and God can use whom ever He wants, to get you to a place that He needs you to be in. Nine times out of ten, God is using that person who hurt you, to bring something out of you, that you never thought was there. God is so amazing, that He will use that mean boss, or unsaved co-worker, as an opportunity for you to teach them and show them the love of Christ; and as a result, not only are you learning to love in spite of how you're being treated, but that mean boss and unsaved co-worker, are being transformed as well because you chose to show love instead of hate.

Trust me, just because you can't see their hearts being renewed, doesn't mean that God isn't at work within them; trust God and just know that He has a plan for your life; and if you find yourself in a situation where you are having a hard time listening to or submitting to someone that God has placed in your life, then ask God for clarity on how to submit to that person; whether that is your teacher, boss, or even your parents. Seek God in everything and remember, God will not change your situation, when He is trying to change you.

DID GOD SAY HE'S YOUR HUSBAND?

Ladies, how can you know if he's the one that God has for you? It's simple; through confirmation. God doesn't just tell or show you he's the one; God will always confirm His word to you through the Holy Spirit. God has proved this to me time and time again. Even when you don't ask for confirmation, God will prove what He said to you is true; and He doesn't have to do this because His word should be good enough. By giving us confirmations, either through His word, or through others, He is showing us how He operates and showing us only a small part of who He is. Another part of God is being faithful and true and wanting to show us just how much He loves and cares for us.

For me, God's Holy Spirit led me to my future husband's YouTube page; and as soon as I heard this man speak, the Holy Spirit came upon me and something inside, just identified with this man's spirit. It really is hard to explain, but I knew that this man; Joseph Jeremiah McConico, was my husband; and after just sitting there watching him talk about God (and cooking), the more I found myself drawn to him. It felt like a tugging in my spirit. It was truly an amazing feeling. Soon after that experience, I asked God simply, *"is Jeremiah my husband? And if so, what do I do?"* God answered me and said, *"Yes. Nothing. I will show him who you are and where you're going."* So, after that word, God had confirmed many times that this man is my future husband. Everywhere I went, I would hear either the name Joseph or Jeremiah; and on top of that, when there times of doubt, that he was my husband, God would immediately allow me to hear my husband's name; either through a tv show, or through a sermon (from OneChurchLA) that I literally watch every day. God is truly amazing and He will never stop amazing you either.

Keep seeking and putting God first and the kingdom, and He will give you the desires of your heart. Truly. And when you seek God for confirmation; keep seeking Him. Don't just ask one time; continually pray and ask the Lord for multiple confirmations until it is clear to you, that the man that God has for you, is for YOU. God Bless You.

About the Author

Melanie K Fernandez is a woman of God living in her purpose and writing for single women who are struggling with their purpose and helping them to prepare themselves for their God-ordained future husbands. She is a single mother of two daughters and is currently pursuing her dreams of becoming a nurse, while writing books and screenplays to encourage women and children in the Lord, and bring them closer Jesus Christ. She resides in North Carolina, but is originally from New York City.

Melanie K Fernandez has also written *"Longing For Him"* and a children's book called *"Bag of Sunshine."*

www.ingramcontent.com/pod-product-compliance
Lightning Source LLC
LaVergne TN
LVHW021626080426
835510LV00019B/2782